midnight meditations

Hymns of Strength and Assurance

Arranged for Piano by
Roger Bennett

Moderate

 **Lillenas** PUBLISHING COMPANY
KANSAS CITY, MO 64141

CONTENTS

Sweet Hour of Prayer

WILLIAM B. BRADBURY
Arranged by Roger Bennett

Slow, with feeling

He Leadeth Me

WILLIAM B. BRADBURY
Arranged by Roger Bennett

Moving along

8

He Leadeth Me

WILLIAM B. BRADBURY
Arranged by Roger Bennett

Moving along

10

Blessed Assurance

PHOEBE PALMER KNAPP
Arranged by Roger Bennett

There Is a Fountain

with

At the Cross

Traditional American Melody
Arranged by Roger Bennett

Moderate

"At the Cross" (Ralph Hudson)

15

My Jesus, I Love Thee

ADONIRAM J. GORDON
Arranged by Roger Bennett

Moderate

Turn Your Eyes upon Jesus

HELEN H. LEMMEL
Arranged by Roger Bennett

Quietly, with emotion

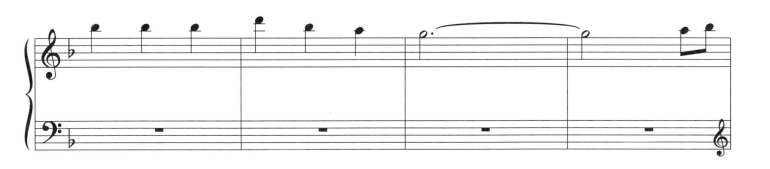

Great Is Thy Faithfulness

with

Abide with Me

WILLIAM M. RUNYAN
Arranged by Roger Bennett

Smoothly

27

*"Abide with Me" (William H. Monk)

The Old Rugged Cross

GEORGE BENNARD
Arranged by Roger Bennett

Reverently

Redeemed

WILLIAM J. KIRKPATRICK
Arranged by Roger Bennett

Lively, in two

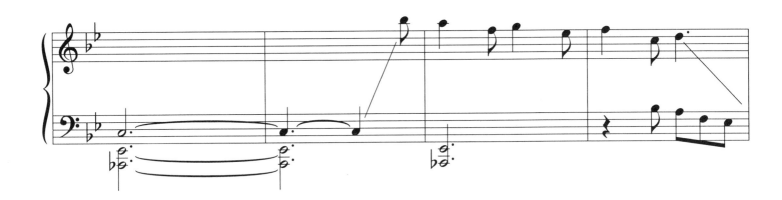

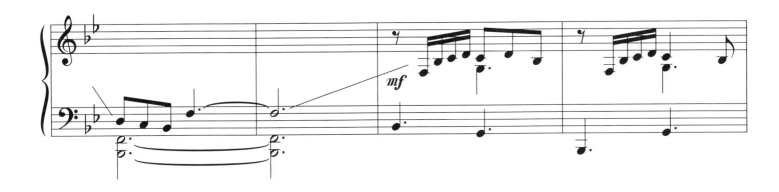

Nothing but the Blood

ROBERT LOWRY
Arranged by Roger Bennett

Calmly

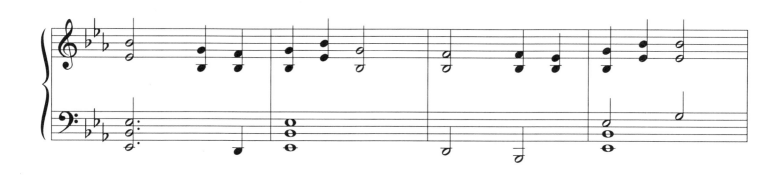

Just As I Am

WILLIAM B. BRADBURY
Arranged by Roger Bennett

Expressively

Just As I Am

WILLIAM B. BRADBURY
Arranged by Roger Bennett

Amazing Grace

Virginia Harmony
Arranged by Roger Bennett

Expressively

He Hideth My Soul

WILLIAM J. KIRKPATRICK
Arranged by Roger Bennett

Smoothly

48

50

Jesus Loves Me

with
Jesus Loves the Little Children

"Jesus Loves Me" by
WILLIAM B. BRADBURY
"Jesus Loves the Little Children"
by GEORGE F. ROOT
Arranged by Roger Bennett

This Is My Father's World

with
Joyful, Joyful, We Adore Thee

Traditional English Melody
Arranged by Roger Bennett

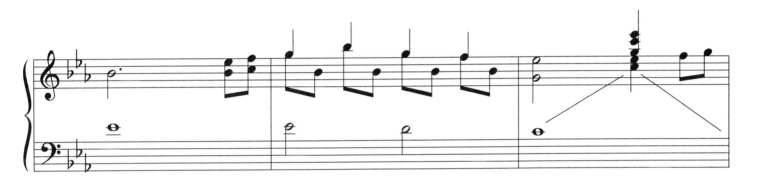

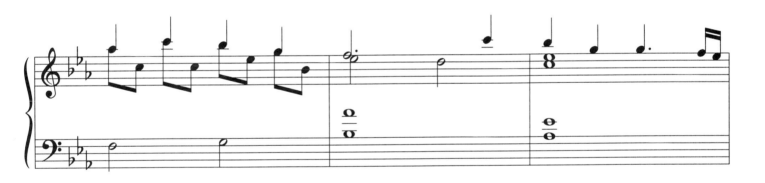

58

*"Joyful, Joyful, We Adore Thee" (Beethoven)

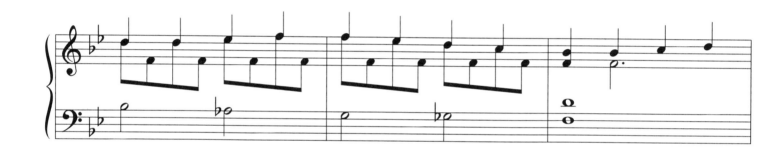